Living Above Average

50 Life Coaching Tips To Help
Change And **Improve** Your Life!

Jeff Crabtree

Living Above Average

50 Life Coaching Tips To Help

Change And Improve Your Life!

By

Jeff Crabtree

Jeff Crabtree is a Life Coach/Motivational Speaker/ Author/Pastor/Consultant. He has been working professionally with individuals and couples now for close to four decades. His belief that personal potential must be discovered and developed is the basis for Living Above Average.

ISBN-13: 978-1722949013

ISBN-10: 1722949015

Endorsements

Jeff is one of the most dynamic and insightful speakers I have been around. I always walk away feeling inspired after listening to, meeting with or receiving personal advice from him. Jeff's genuine, humble approach makes him easy to relate with and trust. Jeff has a special ability to make difficult material understandable, as well as enjoyable. I love his positive approach as well as the way he blends humor with real-life experiences in passionate messages. I am very grateful for the positive impact he has had on my life.

Matt Lubick
Co-Offensive coordinator/wide receiver's football coach
University of Washington

Jeff really gets it. He is a Coach at heart and gets what challenges, motivates and encourages me. In any walk of life, at any stage of growth, in the midst of any challenge, **"Living Above Average"**, speaks truth in a fresh way.

Dale Layer
College Basketball Coach
Mercer University

"Living Above Average" is a must read for anyone who wants to improve the quality of their life, their marriage, their relationships with others, and especially with the creator of the universe.

Ted Schulz
Former PGA Tour Professional
Louisville, Kentucky

I am extremely excited for the release of Jeff's new book **"Living Above Average"**. As a friend and mentor, Jeff has always provided me with valuable insights on how to live life

to its fullest. Now through this book, everyone has the opportunity to hear his words of wisdom which have so often guided me over the years.
Chuck Scheinost
Head Men's Golf Coach
George Washington University

I was once asked the question, "who coaches the coaches?" I, like everyone else, have gone through disappointments, hardships, and struggles. In those dark times as well as others we all need a little coaching. Jeff Crabtree's coaching tips propelled me to live above my problems and not to settle for an average life. It was not by coincidence that our paths crossed and I don't think it is by coincidence that you have this book in your hands! Let **"Living Above Average"** take you places that you may have thought were out of your reach or meant for someone else. It sure has done that for me!
Jeremy Johnston
Head Men's Basketball Coach
Northwest Kansas Technical College

From years of life coaching experience, Jeff has the unique ability to communicate simple truths in powerful, yet practical ways. As Pastor, coach and mentor, Jeff has the expertise to dive into real life issues, wrestle through these circumstances and provide helpful, positive insights to warmly challenge anyone in their journey through life's ups and downs.
Greg Yancey
Former President/CEO – Yancey Foods
Fort Collins, Colorado

I have known Jeff Crabtree since his teen years as a high school athlete and his competitive spirit was off the chart!

As we traveled down life's road together, first as a mentor, then friend, and now follower, I witnessed a transformation from being super competitive to being super compassionate. Each day Jeff reaches out and helps improve other people's life situation. His coaching tips in **"Living Above Average"** are simple, practical, and achievable in helping each of us achieve an above average life.

John Schmidt
Founder/Former Owner- GOJO Sports (1974-2012)
Fort Collins, Colorado

Jeff Crabtree is a passionate man; passionate about his faith, his family and friends. He is also passionate about living an abundant life. In **"Living Above Average"**, he has articulated real life coaching tips that are applicable to all of us and will improve our lives.

Roger Sample
Retired CPA
Fort Collins, Colorado

Everybody talks about "self-improvement". In his new book "**Living Above Average**" Jeff understands change and how to improve your life. This book has wisdom from Jeff's years of living and applying scripture in his personal life. The chapters are short, easy to understand, and to apply. His emphasis upon attitude and positive conversation is essential. Read this book entirely in one sitting or use it as a devotional ... either way, it will change your life!

Grant Edwards,
Founder-Lead Pastor
Fellowship Christian Church
Springfield, Ohio

Jeff is a leader's guidepost. He has always been in the network of those making big things happen. To this leader's network he is always been a sound source of wisdom & guidance. You will find this book a refreshing masterpiece of a Leaders coach & mentor, bringing you up a level! And as Zig Ziglar said "See you at the top!".

Chuck Squeri
Strategic Entrepreneur - Business Leader
Cincinnati, Ohio

For those who truly want to improve their personal life, this is a must-read. Jeff Crabtree is real as he gives life-time tips regardless of where you are in your life. You may apply some or all of the coaching tips found in his book **"Living Above Average"**. Jeff motivates, encourages, and challenges people to an abundant life and expresses ideas to create and maintain incredible relationships. His coaching tips are for everyone!

Bruce Dick
Head Basketball Coach
Resurrection Christian High School
Loveland, Colorado

Quite often the world of coaching is presented through the lens of "do as I say, not as I do". When it comes to Jeff Crabtree, traits of authenticity, integrity and excellence are inseparable. I am grateful for not only the principles in this book, but the author who penned them. Enjoy and APPLY the content!!

Kevin Mark
Vice President of Operations (Texas)
Fellowship of Christian Athletes
Dallas, Texas

Jeff has been a coach to me in so many ways. His careful advice, thought-provoking questions and timely admonitions have pointed me down a path to thriving in all areas of life. I'm deeply thankful to have him as a friend and mentor. I'm confident that his wisdom and insight will serve you the same way as you read this book.

Jason Smith
Fellowship of Christian Athletes Director
Colorado State University
Fort Collins, Colorado

Jeff has done a masterful job blending his vocational experience with his heart for seeing people grow. The Coaching Tips included in this book are vital for anyone who desires to propel forward in life. Jeff helps redefine success and gives practical insight on how you can see your life differently, plow through excuses and obstacles and live the life you were destined to live.

Reza Zadeh
Athletes in Action, National Executive Team
Chaplain for the Denver Broncos
Fort Collins, Colorado

As someone who has been close to me through the darkest of times in my life, I have witnessed first-hand the love this man has for others and his desire to see lives changed. **"Living Above Average"** is not just another book for you to add to your list of things to do. If you will read and truly apply the wisdom provided in this book, I can promise your life will immediately begin to change. I encourage you to read this book and make the CHOICE to Live a **Life Above Average!**
Kyle Crabtree
Son
Plano, Texas

Jeff shares some great insights and nuggets of perspective in his book **"Living Above Average"**. These thoughts and tips have come from his experience and personal journey in life. They are both practical and applicable. You might be surprised at how change and improvement in your own life can come through applying some of the insights and perspectives that he shares. Here's to **"Living Above Average"**!
Kathy Crabtree
Wife of 35 years
Fort Collins, Colorado

Introduction

How is life going for you? Are you making the most of your life? Are you feeling connected and positive in your relationships? Are you struggling with doubt, discouragement, depression or defeat? Is frustration, anger, guilt or unforgiveness hindering you? Do you look at your past and dwell on disappointments and failures? Are you physically healthy? How are you doing in your job or career? How are you doing with your finances? Are you struggling with debt? Are you growing in your spiritual journey? Does the future look cloudy or negative? Do you feel hopeful and positive about your future?

These are some important questions to be considered if you hope to live a successful life and reach your full potential. Our busy, fast-paced culture can keep you from slowing down long enough to properly evaluate and ask the important questions required in regards to **Living Above Average.** Distractions, confusion and a lack of direction can prevent you from learning key tips that will help you in attaining goals and reaching your full potential. These factors can prevent you from moving forward toward a better future!

Extra attention toward current life evaluation, proper goal setting and various **Life Coaching Tips** can vastly change and improve your life. The main reason I decided to write this book is my deep passion to see you live a more exciting, productive, satisfying, positive and successful life. I want you to find yourself **Living Above Average**!

Thoughts from the Author

My professional career working with people encompasses almost four decades. I have worked with individuals from a variety of different backgrounds and life experiences. It seems to me that a majority of these individuals "felt stuck" in one or more areas of their lives. They sought out my professional insight, help, counsel, and direction because they did not know how to get beyond this feeling and condition. I felt compelled to find ways and tips to address this "feeling of stuck" and help motivate them toward a better future.

That is when I discovered Life Coaching. I operated in a counseling paradigm for years. Now I have come to believe the Life Coaching paradigm better enables individuals to process key truths and find key stepping stones that significantly enhance and improve their lives. With a focus on Life Coaching, I have witnessed first-hand how many of my **Life Coaching Tips** encourage, inspire, stretch, give insight, motivate and assist individuals, couples, families and even businesses to reach greater goals and achieve superior results.

I believe the **Life Coaching Tips** you are about to read can catapult you forward toward a more positive future and enable you to reach your full potential! Isn't that what you really want?

Thank you for taking the time to read this book, to invest in yourself and to begin the adventure of **Living Above Average**!

Jeff Crabtree

Getting The Most From This Book

Thank you for taking the time to read this book. In all reality, this is more than a book. It is a guide to help you process tips that can result in you acquiring a better future. I trust that you will read it with a view toward a personal investment in your own life and future. As you well know, it is not what you "know" but what you "apply" that makes the significant difference. If you were to memorize and know each of these tips, but never apply them, they would do you little good. A view toward application will be the key as you read and process through this book. Don't just read this book, interact with it.

So how can you get the most from this book and profitably apply these tips? The following are a few suggestions:

1) Review the Table of Contents to identify any tips that peak your interest.
2) Read the tip.
3) Ask yourself: What does the tip actually suggest?
4) Ask yourself: Is this tip needed for this time in my life?
5) If the tip is applicable for this time in your life, re-read the tip. If not, go to the next tip.
6) Underline or highlight what parts of the tip seem the most significant to you.
7) Identify at least 2 practical steps you can take to start applying the tip.
8) Write down your practical steps or any other notation in the space provided at the end of each tip.

9) Keep applying your practical steps for at least 30-45 days. (This is the normal time for a new habit to become a significant part of life)

I believe that most people live a life below their full potential. Life is a gift you have been given and it is a life with almost unlimited potential! Personal potential must be discovered and developed for it to be realized.

It is my hope and prayer that this book will inspire, encourage and empower you to take many "next steps" toward your goal of **Living Above Average!**

Jeff Crabtree

To schedule an individual Life Coaching Session, Seminar or Worship, please contact Jeff at livingaboveaverage@yahoo.com

Table of Contents

Coaching Tip 1

Make the Most of Life

Do you know what normal or average people do? They often allow the situations and circumstances of life to shape and define who they are. This might sound okay, but in reality, it is a dangerous habit! The very challenging, but harsh reality of life is it provides enough heartbreaks, disappointments, discouragements, traumas, failures, and losses that sometimes it's hard to count.

Have you ever felt that your life was at times difficult, disappointing, meaningless or less than you expected or wanted? Every individual has faced seasons in life where it felt like they couldn't catch a break or that everything seemed to be going against them. In the midst of challenging situations and seasons, why do some people seem to succeed while others seem to fail? Why do some people seem to get all the breaks while others seem to never catch a break? Why do some people seem to come out on top while others seem to be on the losing end of life?

I want to share with you a significant insight. Often times the secret and the difference in these two groups of people is that one group believes that it's not what life makes them, but instead, it is what they make of life. It's about perspective. It isn't as confusing or mysterious as you might think. The key is to not fall prey to the "woe is me", "what's wrong with me" or "victim" mentality. Guarding against this type of thinking can propel you forward to a better future!

It is extremely easy to fall prey to the belief that life is not and has not been fair. This is your battle. A battle you must fight and win. It is a battle against false beliefs and lies. Every situation you face in life can be an opportunity to learn, grow, mature and better yourself. Someone once said, "I am convinced that life is 10% what happens to me and 90% how I react to it". Another saying is "When life gives you lemons, make lemonade." You have a choice and the choice is not what life will make of you, but what you will make of life. Individuals who make the most of life are those who **Live Above Average!**

Coaching Tip 2

Step Beyond Your Limits

Do you desire to become successful and live a full, meaningful and abundant life? Unfortunately, some people stop seeking or desiring greater success due to past hurts and wounds, disappointments or perceived failures. Ask yourself the question "How do I gain success and find a full, meaningful and abundant life?" Many self-help gurus may try and convince you there's a "magic formula". There is no "magic formula"! Success is found in taking one step beyond what you feel is your comfort zone or limit! Far too often you can use comparisons with others to measure your own success. That is a big mistake! You must redefine success in order to achieve it.

Success lies just beyond what you feel you cannot do, cannot give up, cannot sacrifice, cannot touch, cannot afford, cannot allow, cannot consider, cannot comprehend, cannot perceive, cannot dream and cannot apprehend. Notice the common word in each of these phrases is cannot. "Cannot" is the obstacle that is preventing you from being successful! "Cannot" is the biggest hurdle and hindrance that might be holding you back from true success.

Most individuals have self-imposed comfort zones, fears, limits, hang up's or boundaries that they place upon themselves. These can limit their success and ability to have a full, meaningful and abundant life. Success often lies just beyond what you believe or perceive is your limit. If you are willing to challenge yourself to take steps beyond your perceived limit or comfort zone, you will find success. The next time you feel that you are facing your limit, take one more step. That one step can usher you into a brand new realm of success and fulfillment, one you have always desired. Individuals who step beyond their limits are those who **Live Above Average!**

Coaching Tip 3

Cultivate an "I Can" Attitude

Have you ever attempted something and found you were successful? A regular reviewing of your life to identify these successes can be a positive experience. When you are successful in something, it reinforces an "I Can" belief. Our beliefs influence and shape our attitudes and our words. An "I Can" attitude can provide positive motivation for the future. Success in the past leads to a belief that you will have the ability to become successful in the future! Success can breed "I Can" and "I Can" can breed success!

Have you ever attempted something and failed? Each individual can review life and find somewhere they have failed. When you fail at something, it reinforces an "I Can't" belief. An "I Can't" belief can lead to an "I Can't" attitude which can lead to negative words. An "I Can't" belief is unhealthy and can severely diminish positive motivation and momentum. Past failures can tempt you to believe that you will fail again in the future. Failure can breed "I Can't" and "I Can't" can breed failure.

Everyone experiences both successes and failures. Most individuals have felt the daily battles of "I Can" versus "I Can't". Begin to cultivate and nurture an "I Can" attitude about yourself. Battle against and regularly cancel out the "I Can't" attitude. Don't let the past "I Can't" follow you into the future or overpower the "I Can". Understand that you can overcome the "I Can't" attitude. Allow the "I Can" to lead, guide and dominate your present, which will help you to achieve a positive

19

and successful future! Individuals who understand and cultivate an "I Can" attitude are those who **<u>Live Above Average!</u>**

Coaching Tip 4

Establish Positive Self-Talk

Do you talk to yourself? It's okay, you can admit it. Talking to yourself is actually a sign that something is right with you, so let's consider how you talk to yourself. When you talk to yourself, are you positive, kind, considerate, patient, loving and understanding? Or are you negative, rude, impatient, hateful and condemning? The issue is not if you talk to yourself, but how you talk to yourself.

It's sad but very true that most people talk to themselves in a way that they would never talk to someone else. Think of a time when someone spoke to you rudely or inappropriately. How did it make you feel? Did it make you want to be around that person more? Did it bring you closer or farther away from that person? Did it make you angry, resentful, defensive, revengeful or frustrated? If it's inappropriate to talk negatively to another person, isn't it just as inappropriate to talk negatively to yourself?

Can you imagine the positive result and outcome if you could consistently talk to yourself in a positive, kind, considerate, patient, loving and understanding manner? There is great power in words of encouragement and this includes the way you speak to yourself.

If you have fallen prey to negative self-talk, stop speaking inappropriately to yourself! You have control over this. Start respecting yourself by how you talk to yourself. Regular positive self-talk is important and healthy.

Individuals who understand and establish positive self-talk are those who **Live Above Average!**

Coaching Tip 5

Improve Your Focus

Are you a focused individual? If you have difficulty answering this question, maybe this definition will help. Focus, as defined by Oxford Dictionary is "the center of interest, attention, and activity; to pay particular and special attention to."

You have many things vying for your time, attention, and focus. Distractions lurk at every turn and keep you occupied. Whether hobbies, day-to-day tasks, work, or relationships, it's easy to bounce from one thought, idea, project, mission, or goal to another. The result? You lose focus.

We are living in the most over-stimulated culture in human history. The advancements in technology, activities, opportunities, and options have sought to improve the quality of life, but sometimes it's accompanied by negative results. Don't get me wrong. Gadgets, technology, and opportunities have great benefit, but at the same time, they can deter you from what's important and keep you from staying on task.

What about you? Do you find it difficult to say no to all the stimuli and distractions that bombard your thoughts and calendar day after day? If you were to review the schedules of highly successful people, you'd see their ability to stay focused is a strength for success. In a like manner, if you were to review the schedules of individuals who have a difficult time being productive, you'd see their inability to stay focused limits their success.

A majority of individuals live life in such a hurry and with so many distractions that they don't spend enough time and energy improving their focus. It's vital you slow down to improve your focus. Take a few minutes and evaluate how disciplined you are at staying focused during your day. If you conclude you're doing well in this area, great job, keep it up! If you identify your focus as weak or needing improvement, don't give up. Find specific ways to develop this skill. Use a planner to schedule tasks. Periodically unplug from technology. Learn to say "no" to the things that distract you or pull you from what's important. Individuals who improve their focus are those who **Live Above Average!**

Coaching Tip 7

Choose to Overcome

Have you ever tried to avoid a situation and couldn't? No matter how smart, talented, or dedicated you are; you will face situations that are both unavoidable and unpredictable. These situations might be in regards to a relational conflict, an emotional challenge, a financial burden, a family division, a missed goal or a career disappointment. Life can hit you with many unexpected circumstances. In those times, choose to overcome!

How do you choose to overcome? Become thoughtful, strategic, and disciplined to avoid any harmful or destructive situations—the ones within your control. Recognize that you can't avoid all the negatives or pain of life. Make a decision to be someone who overcomes. Too many individuals focus their energy on avoiding rather than overcoming. You can become an overcomer by acknowledging that life will provide you with some negative experiences that can't be avoided. You can either overcome or be overcome. It's that simple.

Look at the lives of those you esteem or who have proved successful. You will see that the outcome of their lives really came down to one choice: They chose to overcome and rise above the circumstances that threatened to overcome them.

Review your past and see where you have overcome certain situations. You will probably discover that you made a conscious decision to fight and overcome. It didn't just happen. Review your past and see where you have been overcome by some situation. You will probably discover in those situations that you made a conscious decision not to fight and the situation overcame you. It comes down to a choice. Make a choice to overcome!

So what challenges or difficulties are you facing right now? Will you overcome them or will they overcome you? It's time you tell yourself you are going to be an overcomer! Individuals who choose to overcome are those who **Live Above Average!**

Coaching Tip 8

Winners Don't "Give-Up", They "Get-Up"

Are you a winner? Winners are defined as those who compete and come out on top. Most people like to win. Winning produces a great thrill and adrenaline rush. Winning is fun and can be quite rewarding, but winning is not always easy. Winning requires focus, hard work, strategy, discipline, perseverance, and momentum. Winning requires a no-give-up attitude, especially in times of defeat and setbacks.

Winners never give up! They have had their fair share of losses and defeats, but they know that it's the getting knocked down that provides the greatest opportunities to get back up. Getting knocked down doesn't consume the winner. A winner is someone who faces great challenges or obstacles and is determined to not be detoured or destroyed by them. Getting up isn't easy, but it is essential for the person determined to be a winner. This determination to get up over and over again is the mentality and practice of a true winner. Winning will require a no-give-up attitude. Winners are seldom developed in the good times, but rather in the difficult times.

You might be facing a difficult challenge or trial right now and you might be thinking or feeling like you want to give up. Don't give up! Stay determined to be a winner. If at some point you do give up, you can always make a decision to simply get back up again. Life will knock you down. It's not how many times you get knocked down that matters, but how many times you get up! The next time you get knocked down, remember it is in the getting back up that you become a winner! Individuals who understand that Winners don't "give-up", they "get-up" are those who **<u>Live Above Average!</u>**

Coaching Tip 9

Think About What You Think About

Have you ever thought about what you think about? Most people never really stop and think about what they think about. Thinking is a bit like breathing, it's so natural that most individuals don't really give it much thought. It really is important for you to think about what you think about! If you learn to track what you think about, you can identify your default thought patterns. This can allow you to begin to make improvements in your thought life.

Begin to identify what your default thought patterns are by tracking what you are thinking about every half hour, hour, half day, full day, and then longer. Once you have tracked thoughts for a specific amount of time, you will discover your default thought patterns. This is important because default thoughts often affect outcomes, either positively or negatively. Individuals think both negative and positive thoughts. Default thinking usually shows a tendency towards one area over the other, either tending to be more negative or more positive. Some individuals seem to spend most of their default time thinking about what is negative, discouraging, painful, judgmental, fearful or depressing. These types of default thought patterns can have negative effects and outcomes. Others seem to focus more on the optimistic, exciting, adventurous, hopeful, joyful, peaceful, or victorious. These types of default thought patterns can have positive effects and outcomes. Studies and statistics reveal that a majority of people fit into the category of negative thought patterns.

Here is an important question for you to answer. Which person do you think has the higher chance of living a happy, meaningful, satisfying and successful life? Those whose thoughts are predominantly negative or positive? Obviously, those with positive default thought patterns!

If you never think about what you think about, you might not be aware of your default thought patterns. It is important to discover your default thought patterns as they can affect your life, either positively or negatively. Changing your thoughts from negative to positive will require focus, work, and a great deal of dedication. It will be well worth the effort and will produce more positive results in your life moving forward. Individuals who think about what they think about are those who **Live Above Average!**

Coaching Tip 10

Choose to Be Positive

Life is about choices. The power in and of your life is found in the choices you make. Life has many up's and down's, with both good and bad days. Every individual has situations that bring them joy or cause them to struggle. It is much easier to be positive about life, others and even yourself when life is going your way. It's on those hard days, or in those challenging situations, that it's easy to become cynical and negative. It is when things are not going well that the choice to be positive becomes so vitally important.

Think of a painful or disappointing circumstance in your past. What choice did you make during this time? Was it positive or negative? If it was positive, I commend you. If it was negative, you are not alone. It's common to choose to be negative when things are not going so well. Did you notice I said, choose? The reality is life is about your choices.

Too many people confuse an emotion with a choice. Choices most often determine your emotions, not the other way around. People often rationalize their emotions and say they have no power over them. Emotions can be controlled, but it requires a choice. If you accept that emotions are choices made, you will have the power to change your choice and thereby change your emotion. When negative, painful or bad things happen to you, you can make a choice to be positive rather than negative.

The key to a successful life is to celebrate the good days and promote the positive emotions you are feeling and experiencing. Success also includes making a choice to hold onto and promote the positives even when life seems down and dark. Life is about your choices. Do not allow your motivation or focus to become negative. Choose today to be a person who focuses on the positives in life! Individuals that consistently choose to be positive are those who **Live Above Average**!

Coaching Tip 11

Don't Follow Distractions

WARNING: Distractions are detours; don't follow them! Have you ever been distracted from pursuing a goal, a dream or a specific result? Our culture and world provide you unlimited distractions. Everywhere you turn, another distraction is inviting you to follow. Distractions, distractions, distractions! That seems to be the name of the game. With a culture dominated by the internet, social media and media in general, distractions have taken a top billing and have become a part of modern-day life.

There are countless distractions from the moment you wake up to the moment you go to sleep. Let me ask you a practical, real-life question. How long is it after you wake up before you log on to view your e-mails, check out your social media or check to see what the latest news headline is for the day? How much time is there between logging off or disengaging from your computer, phone or TV before you fall asleep? These activities are not necessarily bad, but they can become a distraction in everyday life.

Let me shift gears a bit. Can you remember a time when you were driving somewhere and came to a detour sign? The closed road forced you to change directions. How frustrating. Similarly, distractions can provide detours that lead you down a road that can keep you from achieving a goal, dream or specific result. Don't travel down the road of distractions. Distractions can cost you valuable time, energy and effort and can cause you to end up at a destination you don't want.

What are some common things that distract you from pursuing your dreams or goals? Take a quick review of your day or your last couple days and look for distractions that came your way. Begin to view distractions as detours that lead you away from your desired destination. Learn to say no to distractions. Individuals who don't follow distractions are those who **Live Above Average!**

Coaching Tip 12

Every Step in the Right Direction is a Victory

How do you define a victory? Most people define victory in terms of significant events or accomplishments, not the small, day to day positive steps in the right direction. Sometimes in life, you can limit, detour or even derail a more positive future because of how you define or perceive this topic. I believe this to be true in how people often view victory. A narrow perspective limits a person's ability to achieve more success in the present and future. Every step in the right or positive direction is a victory!

What if every time you made a positive step in the right direction, you mentally and verbally complimented yourself on that victory? I believe this practice would help you to feel more victorious. Too many times people get accustomed to being negative about their mistakes and they fail to become positive about their victories.

Take a 3x5 index card, write VICTORIES on the top of the card and place it in your pocket or purse. Each time you take a step in the right direction in regard to any aspect of your life, mark it down on your card. At the end of the day count the number of victories you had that day and celebrate them! You might continue this exercise every day for a week. At the end of the week, count the number of victories you had that particular week. If you will continue this practice for up to one month, you will have established a new mindset and perspective. This will help catapult you to more victories in the future. Individuals who recognize that every step in the right direction is a victory are those who **<u>Live Above Average!</u>**

Coaching Tip 13

Improve Yourself to Improve Others

Have you ever wanted another person to change? Throughout life, we run into people who we would like to see change. It might be a parent, a spouse, a child, a sibling, a boss, an employee, a neighbor or maybe just a good friend. The reasons for wanting them to change are countless. We want them to be more or less of this or that. If they could only be more sensitive, less selfish, achieve more, get along with others better, be happier, less prideful, meet more of your needs... etc. The list goes on! No matter who they are or the reasons you want them to change, people rarely change just to make you happy or because you want them to.

The source of change for most individuals usually comes from 2 sources: they have to or they want to. The best motivation for change is to want to, not have to. Having to change is motivated by pain. Wanting to change is motivated by the pursuit of something better. Obviously, wanting to change is a better motivator than having to change.

How does one get to a place where they want to change? Most times, people desire change when they notice qualities, characteristics, habits, or successes of another individual that are desirable. This desire to be like another individual can initiate change. The pursuit of something better becomes a healthy motivation. It is important to recognize that by making changes to im-prove yourself, you can actually motivate others to im-prove.

Are you willing to be a positive example that will motivate others to change and improve? What areas of your life do you need to change or improve? This might be the time to pause, get out the pen and paper and do the hard work of evaluation. Begin by identifying 3 areas of your life that need some change or improvement. Start developing a plan and some habit adjustments to help you begin to change and improve in the areas you just listed. You are now on your way to making some necessary practical improvements that can motivate others to improve. The next time you find yourself pointing the finger at another person wanting them to change, turn the finger back in your own direction and remember the areas of your own life that need changing. Individuals that are willing to improving themselves to improve others are those who **Live Above Average!**

Coaching Tip 14

Different Speeds for Different Times

Have you ever evaluated the speed at which you live your life? The speed of your life is a very important aspect of living a successful, productive, and joy-filled life. One speed is not always appropriate for the many different challenges, opportunities, situations and chapters of life. You should monitor and adjust your speed as you journey through different situations in life.

To be a safe driver, there will be times when you need to speed up, times when you need to maintain your speed and other times when you need to slow down. The same is true in life. Sometimes you need to speed up; sometimes you need to maintain your speed and sometimes you need to slow down. Utilizing the wrong speed at the wrong time when driving, can place you in danger of a potential wreck. The same is true in life. This simple driving illustration shows us that the concept of speed in regard to life is often misunderstood and underutilized.

Can you think of a time or a situation in your life where you got yourself in trouble because you did not utilize the right speed? Maybe you slowed down when you needed to speed up and you missed a very significant and important opportunity. Maybe you should have maintained your speed, but because you slowed down or sped up, you missed your preferred outcome. Maybe you sped up when you should have slowed down and you made a mess of things. Far too many overlook or misunderstand the great importance for monitoring and adjusting their speed of life.

Review your life and see where your speed either led to positive or negative results. Can you identify some items or aspects of your life currently where you know you need to speed up? What are they? Get going! Can you identify some items or aspects of your life where you know you need to maintain your speed? What are they? Hold steady! Can you identify some items or aspects of your life where you know you need to slow down? What are they? Start tapping the brakes! The person who underestimates the importance of evaluating, monitoring and adjusting their speed can be in danger of a potential wreck! Individuals who understand and apply different speeds at different times are those who **Live Above Average!**

Coaching Tip 15

A New Day, A New Start

Welcome to a new day! Yesterday is over and a new day has dawned. With every new day come's a new start, a new beginning, and a new opportunity. I know that might sound a little cliché, but it is true. Whatever lies before you today, could change your life for the better! A situation may present itself to you today that will enable you to achieve a long-awaited goal. You may meet a new friend today that will bring you long-term and lasting friendship. You may stumble across a truth that empowers you to move closer to your full potential. You may receive a gift that provides you needed inspiration. Each day may present and provide you with countless opportunities that could make your life richer, more satisfying, more rewarding, more content or even more successful. Wow, the power of a new day!

The challenge for most individuals becomes whether or not they can view each new day with hope, perspective, faith, and thankfulness. All it takes is one day to propel your life forward in miraculous and profound ways. Not letting go of the past and what happened yesterday can be a great hindrance to a better and more positive future. Negative thoughts of the past can become detours and roadblocks to the opportunities of a new day.

Whether your past was positive or negative, it is gone. It is over. You can't necessarily duplicate past successes, joys, victories, opportunities or blessings in your future. They were what they were and they are now in the past. Perhaps your past was filled with defeats, heartache, loss, detours, and trauma of all kinds. You should not expect those to necessarily define your future. They were what they were and they are now in the past.

Welcome to a new day, a new start, a new beginning, and a new opportunity. Whatever lies before you today, could change your life for the better! Let go of the past and what happened yesterday. Allow the eraser of yesterday to clean up the whiteboard of your future. Now that the whiteboard is clean, what will you write on it today? Today is a new day! You can write anything you want or desire on the whiteboard of your future. Get busy making the most of your new day and make it something that will make life better and worth living. Individuals who truly recognize that every day is a new start are those who **Live Above Average!**

Coaching Tip 16

Fight the Right Battles

As you consider your life, what are the things that you fight against? It is important for you to clearly identify what you are against. I assume that you have a long list of things that frustrate you, bother you and upset you. These items can cause you to want to fight against them. There is nothing necessarily wrong with this, but make sure what you are against doesn't dominate or negate what you are for.

A second question is what are the things that you fight for? It is important for you to identify what you are for. In this life I'm sure there are things that encourage you, are positive, are good, are uplifting and cause you to want to fight for them.

It is important to think through these questions because you may discover that you are against more than you are for. Most individuals have a host of items that they are both against and for, but they have seldom considered or identified them. Some spend far too much time fighting against things rather than fighting for things. It seems that the current culture can tempt you to be against many things. Be careful, be different and be more positive.

You will never become successful or make a positive impact on our world if you are overly focused on what you are against. You only have a certain amount of time, energy and effort and how you spend it is extremely important. I encourage you to focus most on what you are for. When you fight the right battles, the results are positive, encouraging and uplifting! Individuals who fight the right battles are those who **Live Above Average!**

Coaching Tip 17

Get Rid of Guilt

Have you ever done or said something you regret? Throughout your life, you will probably make countless bad, poor, foolish, negative and potentially destructive decisions. This is just part of the human journey. After you have done or said things that you regret, there is a strong possibility that you felt guilty. Guilt is a painful emotion. It comes when a person realizes that they have violated a personal or moral standard. Guilt is an internal warning signal that one's integrity and character has been violated. Guilt is a normal and natural emotion that every human being will experience and deal with.

Many people ruin their lives, relationships, happiness, careers, opportunities, and future because they never appropriately deal with and overcome their guilt. Guilt not dealt with can become a power that produces poor and negative decisions. You are human and at times will blow it, perhaps way too many times in your lifetime. Continuing to beat yourself up over and over and over again with guilt, will only leave you battered bruised and defeated.

Guilt can be a positive emotion unless it lingers and becomes persistent. If guilt becomes a lingering reality, it can prevent a normal healing process and can create an unhealthy reality. Lingering guilt should be seen as an enemy and be quickly and appropriately dealt with. Don't allow it to guide you down a dangerous or destructive path. If not dealt with, it can become a powerful roadblock to positive, forward momentum and obtaining one's personal potential. The important issue is what will you do when you realize that guilt is present, persistent and lingering in your life? The only prudent answer is to get rid of it! Individuals that get rid of guilt are those who **Live Above Average!**

Coaching Tip 18

To-Do or Not-To-Do

Have you ever done anything and enjoyed the positive results of that choice? Have you ever done anything only to regret the negative results of that choice? Welcome to life! Life is about choices and the consequences of those choices. Life is also a journey and it involves learning. We usually learn best from the consequences we experience that are the results of the choices we make.

In this life, there are "to do's" and "not to do's". It is common for individuals to have "to do" lists, but it is very uncommon to have "not to do" lists. Why do people have "to do" lists, but not have "not to do" lists? I have asked myself that question over and over again and for the life of me, I can't understand why. If it is important to have "to do" lists why isn't it just as important to have "not to do" lists?

I suggest you make a "not to do" list when you make your "to do" list. Here is my point. When you throw caution to the wind and give yourself permission to do things you should not do, you suffer the negative consequences. Sometimes these consequences are hard, hurtful, painful, disappointing and even destructive. Why would you want to keep doing things you should not be doing and continue to suffer the negative consequences? Developing a "not to do" list is a wise and prudent idea.

Practical wisdom knows what to do and what not to do. Wisdom, when applied consistently, allows you to reap the benefits of good decisions and avoid the negative consequences of poor choices. Creating a "not to do" list when you make your "to do" list will enhance and improve your life! Individuals who understand to-do or not-to-do are those who **Live Above Average!**

Coaching Tip 19

Keep the "Main Thing" the "Main Thing"

Most people have heard the saying, – "Keep the Main Thing, the Main Thing." The question you need to ask yourself is how well are you living it out? Are you succeeding or struggling with keeping the "Main Thing", the "Main Thing"?

Let me explore this saying with you a bit. First, what is the "Main Thing"? A "Main Thing" is what matters most to you, your top priority. So, what is the "Main Thing" in your life? What is the most important thing to you or a top priority? Would you say happiness, success, money, possessions, relationships, contentment, joy or personal growth? The first step in keeping the "Main Thing" the "Main Thing" is to determine what that "Main Thing" is for you.

Once you have identified what your "Main Thing" is, now what? Ask yourself "How well am I keeping the "Main Thing" in focus and a top priority?" Then ask "What practical steps do I need to take to make sure I continue to keep the "Main Thing" the "Main Thing"?"

I suggest you establish a regular time of evaluation to concentrate on this topic. In this fast-paced culture, many individuals fail to slow down and have regular times of personal evaluation. This is potentially dangerous and can lead to not keeping the "Main Thing, the "Main Thing". You can't improve what you don't evaluate. Establishing a consistent time to evaluate your life, goals, schedule and the items you have identified as your "Main Thing" is vital. In your time of evaluation, it is also important to identify the distractions and detours that are fighting against your "Main Thing". If you can't or don't identify these, you probably will not be able to keep the "Main Thing" the "Main Thing". When you have identified distractions or detours, make a plan on how to avoid or overcome them. A plan and a set goal are absolutely crucial in keeping the "Main Thing" the "Main Thing". Individuals that keep the "Main Thing" the "Main Thing" are those who **Live Above Average!**

Coaching Tip 20
Your Identity is Who You Are, Not What You Do

Your true identity is in who you are, not what you do! Do you know who you are and are you comfortable with that knowledge? Most individuals are pretty confused about who they are. This is because our culture seems to value performance over personhood. What a tragedy! What makes you unique, special, valuable and incredible does not come from what you do or don't do. It comes from who you are.

You are a very special creation of a God who is magnificent, marvelous and miraculous! I encourage you to take out a piece of paper and write down 10 positive attributes and characteristics that are special and unique to you. This will be a helpful venture, pay significant dividends and benefit your life.

Please note that I did not ask you to write down 10 positive accomplishments. It is not what you have done that makes you so incredible, unique and special, it is who you are. You are one of a kind because you were created that way, not because you earned your identity or worth. Will you be courageous enough to accept that you make our world a better place, simply because you are in it?

Perhaps others, or maybe even you yourself, have defined you by what you have done or have not done, convincing you that you don't measure up or will never be good enough. There couldn't be a bigger lie. What makes you special is you are you! You can blame your failures, disappointments, and hang-ups. I will bring you back to the truth that you are you and that makes you incredibly unique, important and special!

It really does not matter what I think, it matters what you think. If you are having a pity party about your past mistakes, disappointment, and failures, it's time to end the party now. It's time to start believing the truth rather than the lies others have spoken over you or lies that you have believed about yourselves. It's time to stop listening to the culture which is focused primarily on performance, rather than personhood. Our world would be better off and a greater place if people would begin to view themselves and others based on who they are, not on what they do or don't do. Individuals who understand that their identity is who they are, not what they do are those who **Live Above Average!**

Coaching Tip 21

Give the Gift of Understanding

Have you ever felt misunderstood by others? Maybe it was a misunderstanding of communication, intentions, motives, or personal values. It could be that they just didn't understand why you are the way you are. It is hurtful, frustrating, and even painful when someone fails to understand you! It is natural to want and need to be known, understood and accepted.

Have you ever considered that at times you might have failed to understand others? Maybe you did not understand what they were attempting to communicate or possibly you misunderstood their intentions, motives or personal values. Maybe you just didn't understand why they are the way they are.

A lack of understanding can lead to conflict, division, animosity, and resentment in relationships. It can also lead to a person becoming hard, calloused, frustrated, resentful and distant. The end results can be broken relationships, feelings of inadequacy, and struggles with insecurity and inferiority.

If you want to have healthy, fulfilling and positive relationships you will need to strive to be a person who works to improve your ability to give the gift of understanding to others. Human beings long for and desire to be understood. An insightful saying states: seek to understand before seeking to be understood. It takes the character qualities of desire, focus, patient dedication and determination to become a person who is skilled in understanding others. Individuals that consistently give the gift of understanding are those who **<u>Live Above Average!</u>**

Coaching Tip 22

See the Future to Apprehend It

Have you ever slowed down or stopped to consider your future? Most individuals are caught up in the fast lane or the rat race of life, merely focusing on the day-to-day. This hurried and distracted lifestyle can result in failing to consider the future. One of the greatest gifts of this life is the future! The past is the past, it is over, but the future is yet to be realized.

A healthy balance between living in the past and considering the future is wise and imperative. If you don't spend time considering the future, your past might end up dictating more of your future than you want or desire. Approach the subject of your future with great care and intentionality. The way you do that is to carve out specific time to consider, think about, dream and wonder what your future might and could be like. Those that spend time doing this are like gifted and skilled artists who create something brand new out of nothing. A simple idea or dream can become a very positive future.

The future is like a blank canvas waiting for you to draw on it and make it something unique and special. Once you seriously consider the future and see it clearly, then you can get busy to apprehend it! The journey to apprehend the future is not always quick, easy or without challenges, but it is always possible and worth the time and effort. The individual who fails to see the future is the person who walks aimlessly and often disqualifies themselves from a better and more productive life. As the old saying goes, if you aim at nothing, you are sure to hit it. Also, if you don't know where you are going, how will you know when you get there? Consider, see and aim for the future! It is an opportunity you cannot afford to miss! Individuals who understand seeing the future to apprehend it are those who **<u>Live Above Average!</u>**

Coaching Tip 23

Add One Thing to Improve Your Life

Do you want to improve your life? No matter what situations you face; good, bad or indifferent, it should be your hope and desire to want to improve your life. But where do you start? Wouldn't it be nice if there was a formula or a "10 steps to guarantee self improvement" manual? You improve your life by having a sincere desire and a clear roadmap.

At times individuals can make life more difficult and complicated than it needs to be. Perhaps you feel you have to make big decisions, big strides or big advancement to improve your life. In all actuality, it is often the small steps that make the biggest improvements in life. Story after story could be told of successful individuals who made small adjustments which turned out to be the key that led to improvement and greater success in their lives.

If you could "add" just one thing to improve your life, what would it be? It will take some focus, effort, and energy to answer this question. Be realistic in how you answer. After you determine your answer, get busy and do it! You can take control and make significant progress toward improving your life by simply identifying one positive item to "add". If you will consistently answer this one question and then pursue it, you will see positive and steady progress. You will be amazed at how one small addition in your life can make such a big improvement!

The next step is, don't stop! Keep adding that one small thing in your life until it becomes a part of who you are, how you think, how you act and how you go about your daily life! Once this one addition is truly incorporated into your life you will become aware of how your life has improved! Once completed, start again. Ask yourself this same question, answer it and get busy doing it. Before long all of your small additions become multiplications and you will have made significant improvements in your life! Individuals who understand and apply the principle of adding one thing to improve their life are those who **Live Above Average!**

Coaching Tip 24

Subtract One Thing to Improve Your Life

Do you want to improve your life? No matter what situations you face; good, bad or indifferent, it should be your hope and desire to want to improve your life. But where do you start? Wouldn't it be nice if there was a formula or a "10 steps to guarantee self improvement" manual? You improve your life by having a sincere desire and a clear roadmap.

At times individuals can make life more difficult and complicated than it needs to be. Perhaps you feel you have to make big decisions, big strides or big advancement to improve your life. In all actuality, it is often the small steps that make the biggest improvements in life. Story after story could be told of successful individuals who made small adjustments which turned out to be the key that led to improvement and greater success in their lives.

If you could "subtract" just one thing to improve your life, what would it be? It will take some focus, effort, and energy to answer this question. Be realistic in how you answer. After you determine your answer, get busy and do it! You can take control and make significant progress toward improving your life by simply identifying one negative item to "subtract". If you will consistently answer this one question and then pursue it, you will see positive and steady progress. You will be amazed at how one small subtraction in your life can make such a big improvement!

The next step is, don't stop! Keep subtracting that one small thing in your life until it is no longer a part of who you are, how you think, how you act and how you go about your daily life! Once this one subtraction is truly removed from your life you will become aware of how your life has improved! Once completed, start again. Ask yourself this same question, answer it and get busy doing it. Before long all of your small subtractions become multiplications and you will have made significant improvements in your life! Individuals who understand and apply the principle of subtracting one thing to improve their life are those who **<u>Live Above Average!</u>**

Coaching Tip 25

Manage Your Expectations of Others

Have you ever been upset at another human being for not fulfilling your expectations? We often have far more expectations of others than we fully realize. In actuality, our days are full of and consumed with the expectations we have of others. If others would simply fulfill all your expectations, then life would be positive, go smoothly and you would be happy. The problem is, others are not always clear on your expectations or possibly not willing to fulfill them. You can become hurt, angry, resentful and distance yourself from others when they do not fulfill your expectations. The question you need to ask yourself when this occurs is, "Have I clearly and adequately communicated my expectations to the other person?". It could be that you expected incorrectly because you communicated ineffectively. Most relational problems and conflicts are due to improperly managing of expectations.

Here are a few simple steps you can take to ensure better management of your expectations and thus better results.

Identify – Throughout any given day you probably have many expectations of others that you never clearly identify. It is normal and natural to have expectations of others that you don't recognize. Learn to identify when you are having an expectation.

Communicate – How are others to know your expectations if you fail to communicate them or communicate them in a clear manner? Once you have identified your expectations, communicate them clearly.

Clarify – After communicating your expectations, ask the other person if they understood what you tried to communicate. If there is not good clarification, it is likely that a problem will arise. Allowing others to ask questions for clarification is both wise and prudent.

Negotiate – Just because you have identified an expectation, have communicated it and have sought to clarify that the expectation was understood does not mean they have agreed to meet your expectation. Every person deserves the right to negotiate expectations others have of them.

Remind – Once a person has agreed to meet your expectation, they may fail at times to meet that expectation. At that point, a soft, patient and humble review may be in order. Reminders of what they agreed to fulfill are often needed.

Receive and enjoy – The wonderful reality is when expectations are clearly identified, communicated, clarified and negotiated then the expectation can be met. When expectations are fulfilled, the results are often great enjoyment and satisfaction.

Individuals who understand and properly manage their expectation of others are those who **Live Above Average**!

Coaching Tip 26

Learn to Forgive Yourself

Have you ever blown it, made a poor decision or made a mistake that hurt others or possibly even yourself? If so, you are not alone. How did you deal with it? You might be struggling because you have not been able to forgive yourself. Either consciously or unconsciously, you may be holding a grudge against yourself. It is time to take a pause and evaluate if this might be the case. Don't get caught in the trap of feeling that whatever you did was so bad that you must spend a lifetime punishing yourself for it by not forgiving yourself. At times forgiving yourself is easier said than done.

Being unwilling to forgive yourself for past mistakes will severely hamper your ability to move forward to become your best and reach your full potential. Not forgiving yourself is like choosing to be a prisoner in a restricted cell when you have the key to unlock the prison and go free, but you refuse. That would be a foolish and unwise decision.

Forgiveness is not so much a feeling, but a choice that leads to a feeling. When you blow it big time, it is unrealistic to believe you will feel like forgiving yourself. It's more natural to condemn yourself than to exonerate yourself. You must work hard and make a conscious choice to forgive yourself so that in time, the feeling will follow!

Forgiveness is not natural. It is a learned, conscious decision which is often a process. The more you learn to forgive yourself, the easier it becomes in the future. I don't want you live less than your best or miss reaching your full potential simply because you were unwilling to give yourself a break and forgive yourself. Being unwilling to forgive yourself is a roadblock in reaching your best and full potential! Free yourself - Forgive yourself! Individuals who learn to forgive themselves are those who **Live Above Average**!

Coaching Tip 27

The Important Questions of Today

Throughout life, many questions will arise. Some questions will come from your past. Questions like: Why did this or that happen? Why did they treat me that way? Why didn't they understand what I was trying to say? Why was I overlooked for that promotion? Why didn't they love me as much as I loved them? Why did they treat me with such disrespect? Why didn't I see that coming? Why wasn't I able to overcome that? Why was I so foolish? Why didn't I think through that better before responding? Why does life always seem so challenging and difficult? Why, why, why?

On the flip side, some questions will come from your future. Questions like: Will life get better? Will I find someone who really loves me? Will I succeed in my career? Will my marriage be fulfilling? Will my kids turn out well? Will I be healthy and live a long life? Will I have enough money to retire when I want? Will I come to the end of my life and feel successful?

The future has just as many questions as the past. The most important questions are not the questions of the past or even of the future, but the questions of today. Will you make good choices today? Will you love others no matter what? Will you forgive those who hurt you or let you down? Will you live with integrity? Will you be responsible for the tasks set before you? Will you manage your resources wisely? Will you be positive in the face of the negative? Will you use your gifts and abilities to positively influence others? Will you live today with joy and thankfulness? Yesterday is gone, tomorrow is not here yet, so live one day at a time! Individuals who focus on the important questions of today are those who **Live Above Average!**

Coaching Tip 28

Rest When Stressed

Are you stressed? Living in a fast-paced and changing culture can produce constant stress. Our Western culture breeds stress! Some items that can create stress include jobs, school, relationships, divorce, parenting, health issues, finances, preparing for retirement, and caring for aging parents. This world creates a lot of stress. Never before have so many people being medicated for depression and anxiety which are often created by stress. Stress has become epidemic!

How do you deal with stress? Some stress relievers can be negative in nature. Some people may seek to reduce stress with alternate substances such as alcohol or drugs (legal or illegal). Others begin to spend more time involved in unhealthy activities such as excessive amounts of TV, computer or social media. Still, others might fall into overeating, inappropriate relationships or withdrawing from relationships. Any of these responses to stress can be negative. There are a variety of other negative ways in which to deal with stress beyond those listed here. Are you dealing with stress in any negative way?

Again, the question: How do you deal with stress? Some stress relievers can be positive in nature. A helpful suggestion is to go back to the basics and simply rest! We live in a culture that tends to believe that you should be on the go constantly. Go, go, go seems to be today's mantra. No stress reliever in any form is as powerful, energizing, refreshing and effective as rest! A simple definition of rest is to stop work or activity. Rest can include downtime, quiet time, sleep, times of leisure, relaxation, and recreation. There are a variety of other ways in which rest can be found beyond those listed here. Rest is an effective way to deal with stress. How do you rest?

Resting your mind, emotions and body are all vitally important. It's not that individuals don't believe this, they simply don't do it or they don't do it on a consistent basis, but you can. The main point is to get more rest! Rest will help you deal with the stress of a hectic and busy life. Individuals who rest when stressed are those who **Live Above Average!**

Coaching Tip 29

Ask Questions Before You Criticize

We live in a world that is super-charged with criticism. Everywhere you turn it seems that criticism is in full force. We can be overcome with critical attitudes and a host of other negative emotions. We all have fallen prey to the influence and power of these at one time or another, whether on the giving or the receiving end.

Have you ever been unfairly criticized? I'm sure you have. Have you ever unfairly criticized? I'm sure you have. What positive results came from someone criticizing you? What positive results came from you criticizing another? The answer is sobering. Nothing! Nothing good, positive or redeeming comes from criticism. So why do we criticize? Because we are human and it comes naturally to all of us. Since we can't stop being human, it means that we must learn to overcome our natural tendency to criticize. How do you overcome your natural tendencies to criticize? You learn to ask questions first. By asking questions, you seek to gain information that you don't have which often leads to the criticism.

For instance, when you have been criticized, the person criticizing you in most cases did not have all the information about you or your situation. They may not really know you and they may not know what you were seeing, thinking or feeling. The lack of information led them to criticize you. If they would have asked questions and gained more information, their attitude and actions would most likely have been different! In like manner, you can fall prey to criticizing another. You probably didn't have all the information about that other person or their situation. You most likely failed to understand what they were seeing, thinking or feeling. Your lack of information led you to criticize them.

Learn to ask questions before you give yourself the freedom to criticize others. When you are tempted to criticize, slow down and ask these important questions - What is that person seeing, thinking or feeling which is causing them to do, act or say things that lead me to want to criticize them? Simply pausing and asking these questions can be enough to put the brakes on your natural desire to criticize. When you are unable to answer these questions on your own, you may need to pose those questions to the person you are about to criticize. At this point, it might be helpful for you to remember the old saying – do unto others what you what them to do to you. If you don't want to be criticized unfairly, don't criticize others unfairly! Individuals who ask questions before they criticize are those who **Live Above Average!**

Coaching Tip 30

Look Up When You're Down

Have you ever felt down or discouraged? There are and will be many situations and seasons in life that will get you down. When you are down, how will you respond? For many, being down becomes a habit, a persistent perspective, a way of life and it robs them of the opportunities and quality of life that are available.

What can you do when you feel down and discouraged? I suggest you look up! It is not as easy as it seems or sounds, but taking positive action is important. Staying down is not a positive solution and it certainly won't improve your situation.

When I say "look up" it can take on a variety of applications depending on your personality, opinions, and perspectives. First, it can be literal. When you are down, physically look up. Looking up allows you to change your view physically. It can help you notice the broad horizon, the beauty of the sky, birds soaring through the air, clouds with the ability to bring moisture to the earth, or perhaps even a storm expressing its awesome power. Looking up can bring into view the beauty of a moonlit night or stars that shine so brightly that they light up the night sky. Physically looking up can bring a whole new perspective, which can be both healthy and healing. Having a limited perspective of our small world can be a hindrance. You can look up to bigger and broader perspectives.

Second, looking up might be that you have to look for answers and solutions in places and with people you have not previously looked. Looking up could mean that you accept that you cannot handle or battle life by yourself or without the help of others. There are just some situations and seasons where you have to move beyond your comfort zone and search out other sources to help you.

Third, looking up could include tapping into faith in a new way. Faith, when neglected or ignored, loses its power and influence to aid you. Once faith is recognized and activated, it has the ability and power to make a positive difference in your life. Some situations and seasons of life need greater faith to be activated. Look up when you are down! Individuals who look up when they are down are individuals who **Live Above Average!**

Coaching Tip 31

Refocus When Discouraged or Disappointed

No doubt you have faced many discouragements and disappointments in life. These are a part of the human journey. The real issue is not whether you can avoid these realities, but how you handle them when they occur. As the old saying goes "It's not what happens to you, but how you respond that makes the significant difference".

Do you find yourself saying "Why me?", "Life is not fair!", "Why not others?", "I can't ever seem to catch a break!" or "Bad things always seem to happen to me?" If so, then it's time to refocus. Do any of the following emotions have a negative impact on your life and attitude? Anger, resentment, revenge, criticism, cynicism, jealousy, or persistent negativity. If so, you could forfeit your opportunity to be successful in the future! It's time to refocus.

Believing and preparing for great opportunities in the future will help you overcome the discouragements and disappointments that you have faced. They key is not denying your perspectives, but redirecting them. This is where refocus comes into play. What does it mean to refocus? Refocus is adjusting what you are focusing on, changing from a negative focus to a positive focus. It includes telling yourself that something better is coming from all the discouragements and disappointments. It is looking back to see past success from previous difficult times. It is accepting that personal growth will be achieved through the difficulties in life.

Some of the greatest leaders, thinkers and world chang-ers of human history were those who faced great dis-couragement and disappointment. Each of them used refocus toward a positive perspective to propel them to greater realities during those difficult times. If you are stuck or you are being detoured by current discourage-ments and disappointments, it is time to refocus. Indi-viduals who refocus when discouraged or disappointed are those who **Live Above Average!**

Coaching Tip 32

Overcome or Be Overcome

You really only have two choices in life—to overcome or to be overcome. Each day is filled with many situations, decisions, struggles, opportunities, and responsibilities. Within each of these, you can either overcome or be overcome. Life includes good days and bad days. There will be successes and failures. There will be up's and down's. There will be positives and negatives. There will be dreams fulfilled and dreams dashed. There will be captured opportunities and lost opportunities. There will be times of great joy and great sorrow. Life will throw the best and the worse at you. The question is not what will come your way, but rather what will you do with what comes your way? With each new day, new situation, new experience and new decision you will have a choice to make. Will you overcome or will you be overcome?

Your decision will determine your outcome. Far too many individuals allow their situations and circumstances to determine whether or not they overcome rather than actually making the decision for themselves. Life is about choices. If you allow yourself to be overcome, you will be overcome. Failure results in more failure because individuals refuse to learn how to choose to overcome. If you choose to overcome, you will be an overcomer. Success results in more success because individuals learn to overcome.

The sad reality is that far too many individuals are overcome rather than overcome. That does not have to be you! Some individuals face all kinds of situations, issues, and realities that cause them to stop developing into a better person. The result is that they are overcome. Other individuals face the same kinds of situations, issues, and realities, but it causes them to develop into a better person. The result is that they overcome. It is all about choices. Will you choose to overcome or will you be overcome? No matter what comes your way or what you face, let it develop you into a better person and you will become an overcomer. Individuals who chose to overcome rather than be overcome are those who **Live Above Average!**

Coaching Tip 33

Release Your Control

We love to be in control, don't we? We often try and control people, situations and circumstances to secure what we want or hope for. The reality is that much of life is outside your control. Let me state the obvious: You cannot always control life, others, specific situations and circumstances. Can you remember a time you tried to control a person or a particular situation and found yourself frustrated or angry when you could not control them or it? Frustration and anger are stealers of joy, peace, contentment, and stability. These negative emotions can lead to negative results.

The desire for or need to control is often rooted in past hurts, pain, rejection, disapproval and disappointment. As a result, we may think that if we can control people, situations, and circumstance, we can then protect ourselves from experiencing these painful, negative emotions. This subtle and often subconscious motivation is the source of an inappropriate tendency to control.

How do you release your control in regards to many of life's issues? You release the expectation, that you should have the right to control life's issues or other people! This is an important first step, but it is harder than you might first think. It takes focus, energy, courage and personal discipline. When you release your desire and right to control, you can take life on its terms. When you can accept life on its terms, you can then be free to respond with integrity and wisdom. Integrity and wisdom will always be needed for a successful life! Less need of control, less frustration, and less anger will result in a better, more positive and more meaningful life! Learn to allow life to happen rather than always needing to be in control. Individuals who release their control are those who **Live Above Average!**

Coaching Tip 34
Determine Directions to Your Destinations

Life is a journey. On that journey, it is important that you establish clear and specific destinations. A destination may be a specific goal, desire or achievement. Have you thought through and determined some specific destinations that you want for your life? Most people get up every morning and merely maintain what comes their way. As the old saying goes, if you aim at nothing you are sure to hit it. If you don't know where you are going, you are sure to end up detoured. The truth is, many people do not achieve or arrive at many of their desired destinations. It does not have to be that way for you!

Once you determine specific destinations, recognize that there are usually many routes, roads, and pathways to those destinations. With this in mind, it is crucial for you to understand and determine specific directions you will follow to arrive at your desired destinations. Recently, while traveling, I picked up my rental car and they handed me a map. Though I appreciated the gesture and kindness, I knew I would just drop it in the trash. I was convinced I knew where I was going and how I was going to get there. For some strange reason, I decided to review the map and guess what; I found a different and better route to my final destination. The map became a great source of assistance to me in deciding which route was the best one for me to take.

Have you had something or someone try to provide you understanding on how to get where you were going and you simply passed it off as unimportant? You were confident that you knew where you were going and how to get there. Have you ever refused guidance or advice when making a significant, directional decision toward a specific destination? Could it be possible that there are better routes to your destinations that you are unaware of? To get the most from your life, spend some time clarifying your specific destinations, as well as the best directions to get you there safely, timely and efficiently. Individuals who determine directions to their destinations are those who **Live Above Average!**

Coaching Tip 35

Think of Others More

Every person has a total of 1440 minutes in each day, which is the equivalent of 10,080 minutes per week. How much of that time will you spend thinking of others, rather than yourself? Most people don't give much thought to this question. Most are consumed with thinking about themselves from the time they wake up until the time they go to sleep. What about you? The truth is, most individuals are overly self-focused. We should learn to think of ourselves less.

Any successful individual knows they must budget their time like they budget their finances. They allocate a specific amount of the time in their day and week toward that which provides the greatest opportunity to increase productivity. In this case, allocating a specific amount of each day and week toward thinking of others should be a top goal and priority for you. The goal to increase the amount of time you spend on thinking of others is simply your decision. Without a clear and firm decision to think of others, it probably won't happen. Leaving it to chance or feelings means it probably will never become a reality!

After a clear and firm decision has been made, a specific plan needs to be determined. No plan usually results in no progress. Before you get consumed with the projects and business of your day, determine a specific amount of time that you will spend on thinking of others. It may start out with a small amount of time, say 10-15 minutes, but that's a start. After determining how much time you will focus on others, then determine some specifics on how you will practically accomplish this. Plan your work and work your plan. Ask yourself "How can I be a blessing to someone else today". You might determine to give someone a call, write them a note, purchase them a specific item, make time in your calendar to meet or listen to them, or it might be saying a short prayer for them. Do something unexpected.

Once setting aside time to think of others becomes a habit, you may decide to devote more time to this each day or week. In doing this, you have the opportunity to refocus, moving from yourself to others. This is a very positive activity! If each person in our world determined to spend a specific amount of time each day thinking of someone else, our world would be positively impacted! People would be happier, more self-fulfilled, encouraged and inspired to live a full, meaningful and abundant life. Individuals that think of others more are those who **Live Above Average!**

Coaching Tip 36

Choose Positive Thoughts

Life is all about your choices. Each and every day you make choices about how you will live. Choices are the fabric of being human. From the moment you are born until the moment you die, you will make choices. From the moment you wake up in the morning until the moment you go to sleep, you will make choices. Your ability to make choices is one of the greatest gifts you have in life. Without choices, you would be captivated by a very cruel kind of robotic imprisonment.

Have you ever slowed down or stopped to consider that you have choices in regard to your thoughts? Many people act and live like they have no choice over their thoughts. This is not only a falsehood, but is potentially dangerous as well. I am not saying you can totally control every thought that comes into your mind, but that you have a choice on how you respond to every thought. Every human being will face on a regular and consistent basis, both positive and negative thoughts. The choice of how you will respond to every thought is up to you and under your control.

If you have a positive thought that comes to your mind, you will have a choice on what to do with that thought. You can accept it, enjoy it, focus on it and even expand it or you can ignore it, negate it, fight against it or even reject it. The same is true with a negative thought. If you have a negative thought that comes to mind your mind, you will have a choice on what to do with that thought. You can accept it, enjoy it, focus on it and even expand it or you can ignore it, negate it, fight against it or even reject it. You have a choice with all of the thoughts that come to your mind, both positive and negative! Don't believe or buy into the lie that you have no choice, power or control over your thoughts, you do! Individuals who choose positive thoughts are those who **Live Above Average!**

Coaching Tip 37

Change is Inevitable

We live in a world of change! Seldom do situations, circumstance or people remain the same without some type of change. Change is common and it is inevitable. For some, change seems positive, adventurous, exhilarating and thrilling! For others, it seems negative, scary, threatening and unwanted. Ask yourself the question: "Do I see change as positive or negative?" Your answer is vitally important and may be the difference between a future of fulfillment and greater success or a future of frustration! As the old saying goes, people don't change unless they want to or have to.

Let's assume you allow change to guide you, what will that mean? It will mean that you are ready to embark on an adventure of a lifetime where new opportunities and potentials exist. Change can and will take you places that self-protection would prevent you from going. It will take you to places where the hurts, disappointment and the failures of the past are not welcome. Change will cause you to risk like you have never risked before. Change will cause you to stretch in such a way that you will come to acknowledge that you have greater stamina and potential than you ever realized. Change will cause you to trust like you have never trusted before and will propel you upward and forward in a positive manner. Change can help you find and fulfill your deepest longings and potential.

If you choose to fight change, what will that mean? It will mean that you will fight a battle that in all reality cannot be won. You will not prevail when you view change as an enemy! Those who fight change are often dominated by a need to control life, people, and circumstances. Fighting change is like swimming upstream against the natural current. Fighting change will cause you to be farther out of touch with the world, others and even yourself. Fighting change is the ultimate denial of a reality of life. The choice is yours, will you make a positive choice to let change guide you to something better or will you fight it? Individuals who accept that change is inevitable are those who **Live Above Average!**

Coaching Tip 38

Success - The "Who" and The "What"

Western culture has often attempted to define what success is. Success in this culture has often been defined for the most part about "What". What you gain, what you acquire, what you own, what job you have, what you achieve, what influence you have, what others think about you, what you look like and what you appear to be. While some of these items are certainly important and worthwhile, they also can create a shallowness and externalism that is potentially dangerous. If a person defines success merely by "What" they have, own, look like or achieve it can provide a detour that can erode true success. "What" does not always provide or pay off in the way you might expect!

Success should also include "Who". Who you really are when no one is looking, who admires and respects you, who you admire and respect, who calls you a friend, who you call a friend, who can count on you when their life gets challenging, who you can count on when your life gets challenging, who enjoys being around you, who you enjoy being around, who is a positive influence on you, who you are a positive influence on, who trusts you and who you trust. "Who" is vital for life's success! Success includes "Who" and "What".

I have met people who have obtained above average possessions, popularity and positions, but have failed to find and enjoy true success. On the other hand, I have met people who have little or an average amount in the way of possessions, popularity or positions, but are extremely successful. Their success is based upon the positive relationships they have and enjoy. I trust you are catching the idea and focus on "Who".

Seek to evaluate "Who" and "What" when you consider the definition of being successful. I believe that in most cases true success in life is about attaining the right "Who" as much as the right "What". You would be wise to make sure the "Who" in your life is as important if not more important than the "What". In a world of "What", make it also a world of "Who"! Individuals who understand success is about the "Who" and the "What" are those who **Live Above Average!**

Coaching Tip 39

Focus on "Resolution" Rather Than "Conflict"

Having a conflict is both human and natural! There is potential for conflict anytime two unique and different individuals interface. You will find a variety of world-views, values, perspectives, hopes, dreams, likes and dislikes in the people that you encounter. Individuals are different and with differences can come potential conflict. When conflict arises, it can be tempting to focus on and become consumed with the conflict itself. Conflict is one person believing their perspective and views are correct while the other person is in the wrong. Most people love to be right and can have a difficult time accepting when others don't agree with them. This can provide an environment for conflict.

As long as the focus is on the conflict, the resolution will remain unresolved. Individuals who remain engaged and fighting the battle of conflict, decrease their chances for a successful resolution, short and long-term. Successful resolution of conflict requires that the conflict not be the major focus, but instead the resolution is the main focus.

Here are five helpful steps to move toward conflict resolution.

1. Listen – pay attention
2. Hear – understand the other person
3. Ask questions – clarity
4. Validate – everyone has a right to their view
5. Agree or agree to disagree

Think about a conflict that you have recently experienced or one that you are currently engaged in. Ask yourself if the focus was/is more on the conflict or on the resolution. Successful people make a conscious choice to move from conflict to resolution! When resolution becomes the focus and priority, success in that conflict is usually close at hand. Growing in your skill and ability to resolve conflict effectively is a significant trait of highly successful individuals! Individuals who focus on "Resolution" rather than "Conflict" are those who **Live Above Average!**

Coaching Tip 40

Learn to slow down

Are you living a fast-paced life? Are you always busy, on the go, consumed with another activity and project? If you answered "yes", you are in good company. Most individuals live in the fast lane. It seems as most people are always in a hurry to get somewhere, complete some project or get something else accomplished. Our culture has bought into the idea and belief that hurry makes you successful or at least makes you look successful. People that are caught in the hurry mentality seem to often be exhausted, stressed out, on edge, uptight and burned out. These symptoms are the results of a hurry mentality. Most people seek to cram as much as possible into their lives which keeps them on the path of hurry, hurry, hurry.

Is your life characterized by hurry, hurry, hurry? If so, is it producing the results you desire? Are you peaceful, content, satisfied, joyful and relaxed? If not, maybe you need to deal with the hurry mentality. Unfortunately, some people stay in the hurry mode because they are scared of what life would be like if they slowed down. They are and have become addicted to hurry and without it, they feel they might not be able to function adequately.

Learn to slow down, "stop and smell the roses", and reduce the fast pace that controls so many in this current culture. When you do, you'll begin to appreciate the people, relationships, opportunities, and blessings in your life. Individuals who have not allowed the addiction to hurry to consume them are often happier, more satisfied and more content. They have said no to the hurry mentality and they have adopted a slower pace of life. If you can begin to eliminate some of your hurry, you can experience a greater quality of life! Individuals who learn to slow down are those who **Live Above Average!**

Coaching Tip 41

Adjust Your View of Obstacles

Have you ever faced an obstacle? Life is filled with many different types of obstacles. By definition, an obstacle is, "something that blocks, prevents or hinders progress". Your obstacles may be preventing personal growth, skill development, relational health, career advancement, financial stability, or a host of other life events. When an obstacle blocks your way, it can be very disappointing and frustrating. If you are not careful you can begin to believe that the obstacle is communicating to you that your goals are wrong, improper, inappropriate or just not attainable. Sometimes obstacles are life's way to tell you that you are on a wrong path, but often an obstacle is simply communicating there may be a better pathway or avenue to your goals.

Some people do not handle obstacles well. They continue to hit the same obstacle over and over again. Finally, they get frustrated and quit pursuing whatever goal they had been trying to obtain. Maybe your goal is good, adequate and correct, but the obstacle is simply life's way of saying there is a better or more profitable pathway to your goal. Obstacles are not always negative. Many obstacles can be viewed as positive and helpful. Life is about gaining wisdom and understanding from the situations we face. What if an obstacle doesn't mean no, it simply means a different way?

Can you identify at least 3 major obstacles that you are currently facing or have faced in the last month? How long have they been obstacles? What created these obstacles? Are the obstacles major or minor in scope? Do you see how you can overcome these obstacles? Are these obstacles trying to reveal to you that there is a better course and pathway to your goal? Could these obstacles become positive in the long run, even though they may currently feel negative, frustrating or wrong? Maybe your current obstacles are an opportunity to pivot, to choose a different or better path toward your goal. Many obstacles you face can work for you rather than against you. Individuals who learn how to adjust their view of are those who **Live Above Average**!

Coaching Tip 42
Develop a Desire to Listen to Others

We live in a world and culture of talk. Talk, talk, and more talk. It seems that most people believe that talk is the most important aspect of life. Talk is important, but there is something that is as important as talking. Listening! Listening often times has more importance and merit than talking!

In our world, many individuals are in need of someone to listen to them. Talk to a local psychiatrist, psychologist or pastor in your area and I am sure they will confirm that a large portion of their clientele or congregation, is seeking someone to listen to them. In a world that is extremely busy, distracted and self-consumed many people feel that they have few individuals, if any, that will spend the time to listen to them. I believe this is a modern day tragedy and an epidemic. Every human being deserves the right and the opportunity to be prioritized in such a way that someone listens to them.

Do you desire for someone to care enough about you and what you are going through that they would listen to you? It seems that most everyone is so busy and interested in their own lives, they have little or no time to focus on others. I don't know about you, but I have a desire and need for others to listen to me. I also have an earnest desire and passion to listen to others. I want to serve others, my culture, and world by being someone that will listen! Will you join me in this goal?

One of the first steps to apply this tip is to evaluate who in your life seems to need a listening ear. Once you identify that person, invite them to talk to you. Ask them questions and listen to what they have to say. As you develop a desire to prioritize listening to others, I am confident you will find great fulfillment and satisfaction. You will provide a needed and scarce reality in our current culture. Individuals who develop the desire to listen to others are those who **Live Above Average**!

Coaching Tip 43

Establish and Maintain Healthy Expectations

Expectations are a part of everyday life. You will naturally have expectations of others and others will naturally have expectations of you. You will also have expectations of yourself. It is natural to have these expectations.

Several potential problems exist in regards to expectations. First, the reality of expecting certain things of others. Unmonitored, you can inadvertently let your expectations of others run wild. Without effective monitoring of these expectations, you can allow them to begin to rule your daily reality. If you are not careful, you can expect others to be or do what you want, without much sense of reality. At the core this propensity for out of control expectations is selfishness. This type of attitude and behavior leads to hurt and disappointment when expectations aren't met. This is because reality does not always correspond with your out of control expectations.

Second, you can allow expectations that others have of you determine who you are and what you do or don't do. If you do this, you can fall prey to attempting to please others. With this compelling need to please others, you can lose a sense of your self-worth, value, and self-fulfillment. Becoming consumed in attempting to please others, you limit your time, energy or effort to achieve your own goals, dreams, and expectations.

Third, you can allow unrealistic expectations of yourself to become dominant, distracting and discouraging. Many people struggle as they often set their expectations of themselves too high. If this happens and you regularly fail to meet your own expectations, the results can be a "failure mentality" which is harmful and unproductive.

The expectations you have of others, they have of you and you have of yourself can become too excessive and dominate. It is vitally important that you regularly establish and maintain healthy expectations. Learning to discipline yourself to take control over your expectations allows you to be on your way to a happy, productive and successful life. Individuals who establish and maintain healthy expectations are those who **Live Above Average!**

Coaching Tip 44

Dream Really BIG

Do you ever underestimate the impact you can make in this world? Have you ever noticed how easy it is for you to think small, not really big in regard to your future dreams? A dream is potential for a future reality, something hoped for, often something that is difficult to attain or far removed from your present situation. What is your dream or your dreams? Are they really big? What is or has kept you from pursuing it or them?

Have you ever thought, "Who am I that I can do something really big, great or even world-changing?". Perhaps you have faced times and situations of discouragement, defeat, failure and missed expectations. When this happened, did you fall prey to doubt, fear, and disbelief? You can easily believe these emotions and realities disqualify you from your big dreams. They don't! If you believe they do, then today is a great day to stop believing the lie. You can start believing a new truth that you can dream and accomplish really big dreams.

Every new day provides you with choices. Begin today to dream really BIG. Take a moment and write down 3 really BIG dreams that you would like to accomplish in your future. Now review them. Once you have your really BIG dreams identified, begin to identify some small steps towards your dream(s) and then get going! What do you have to lose? With these steps, you may encounter more disappointments or perceived failures, but so what! The other side of possibility is that you may achieve those really BIG dreams! It is certainly worth the risk. Don't give yourself any more excuses that keep you from pursuing your dreams! Give yourself permission to dream really BIG! Individuals who dream really BIG are those who **Live Above Average**!

Coaching Tip 45

Be Authentic in An Artificial World

The American culture seems to be fascinated with appearances and is often gripped by the artificial. The word artificial simply means not real. The opposite of real is fake. Our culture is infatuated with looking good, performing right, projecting the best side with an extreme focus on the externals of life. Appearance has often become more important than reality. There are countless illustrations of this in the entertainment industry where actors and actresses are made to look elite and superhuman. The result of this is that they become glamorized. What is seen on TV or in the movies is not the real, authentic person. It is fake, artificial. This is and has become a national epidemic.

Stroll through the magazine section at any store and you'll see flawless faces on the covers. Discontentment and low self-esteem surface as you compare yourself to these airbrushed models. The somber danger in all of this is that you can confuse what's artificial with what's authentic and lose your grip on reality. The more you pursue the world's standard, the more you drift from authenticity. This distracts you from living up to your full potential. This perspective damages your ability to embrace who you are as a unique, special and awesome individual. It can cause emotional damage. The difference between who you are authentically and who you are artificially is an indicator of your mental wellness. It is dangerous to get caught up in and addicted to the artificial.

How much of your life is spent pursuing the artificial you, rather than the authentic you? If a large portion of your life, energy, self -worth and self-esteem are based on the artificial rather than the authentic, it's time to address it and change. You can't change something if you don't first accept it. Today can become a great day as you begin pursuing the authentic which can have a great influence and power over your life. There is a desperate need in our culture for a resurgence and revival of authenticity. Authenticity enables you to live and enjoy a much healthier and balanced quality of life. Will you continue to be influenced and follow the artificial or will you determine to live and be a positive example of authenticity? Individuals who are authentic in an artificial world are those who **Live Above Average!**

Coaching Tip 46

Never Give Up

Can you think of a time or a situation where you wanted to give up? Did you? If you wanted to, but didn't, are you glad now that you didn't? Giving up does not solve anything and is not productive or positive in any way. If you did give up, do you regret it? Do you wish you made a different decision? Do you wish you could turn back the hands of time? A successful life is about learning important life lessons. Learn from your mistakes and move on. The past is the past, but the future is still yet to be lived.

This world and culture often propagate the message of "give up" if things are not going your way, if it gets too tough, if it's going to cost too much or things do not come as easily as you wanted or expected. These subtle or sometimes blatant messages can have an influence on you. They can call out to you in some of the most difficult and vulnerable times of life. If you are not careful, you can begin to listen to these messages and they can sway your decisions more than you realize. Battling the temptation to give up is a real fight. When you fight through the "give up" temptation, you will be glad you did. When you yield to the "give up" temptation, you are almost sure to regret it.

Maybe you are currently facing or will soon face a situation where the message "give up" becomes tempting. Will you yield to it? Please don't! The temptation to "give up" usually ends worse than you think. Giving up does not solve anything and is not productive or positive in any way. Can you identify some important lessons you learned from not "giving up" or lessons from when you did "give up" in the past? How can you apply them today and in the future? Individuals who determine they will never give up are those who **Live Above Average**!

Coaching Tip 47

Live to Make a Positive Difference

Are you making a positive difference in this world? This is an important question to ask yourself periodically. In the midst of busyness and hectic schedules, it's easy to skip over this important question and not evaluate the impact you are making and can make in this world.

If you answer yes, can you identify specific ways that you are making a positive difference? Identifying these brings clarity and encouragement. If you answered no, maybe you have underestimated your ability to make a positive difference. This coaching tip has a twofold purpose. First, to bring this question into focus and allow you to ponder it. If it never gets on your radar screen, it can never help you to evaluate and make the difference that it is intended to make. Second, it is to encourage you to recognize that you can make a positive difference thus making this world a better place. Life is all about choices! Will you choose to make a positive difference?

I've noticed how quickly people underestimate their ability to make a positive difference in the world. Do you? If so, it could be due to feelings of insecurity, inferiority, past failures, lies you have believed about yourself or a host of other causes. The simple truth is that if you don't think you can make a positive difference in this world, you won't! It's all in your thinking and choices. If you think you can, you can!

Be aware that you can get sidetracked if you think you have to do something huge, large, marvelous, miraculous or earthshaking in order to make a positive difference in this world. This is wrong thinking! You can make a positive difference by all the small choices, actions, activities, and decisions you make day to day. If you are one of those people who has underestimated your ability to make a positive difference, make a choice to stop believing the lie and get busy. You can make this world a better place if you choose to! Individuals who live to make a positive difference are those who **Live Above Average**!

Coaching Tip 48

Stay Determined – Press On

In life, there will be chapters, seasons or situations that are challenging. It could be a relationship, job, finances, health or even emotions that are creating difficulty. It is as if there is a "headwind", something that seems to provide resistance to forward progress and interferes with the ability to reach desired goals. In these times it is very easy to get distracted and become focused on the challenge, obstacle or problem. If you become overly focused on the"headwind", it can cause you to get discouraged. Think of a time in your life when things did not go the way you had wanted or hoped for. Maybe it is something going on now. What was or is the "headwind"? Has the "headwind" become the focal point instead of the goal or desired result? When this happens, you can begin to get distracted. If you stay distracted, discouragement often follows.

I have enjoyed running for the past 40 years. I enjoy the weather, scenery and the health benefits. Not too long ago I went for a run. On this particular day, I began to experience some fairly strong headwinds. I do not like to run in the wind, especially headwinds. As I continued to run, I realized that I became overly focused on the wind. It became apparent that I was distracted from the run, the beautiful weather and the stunning scenery. The more I focused on the headwinds, the less I enjoyed the run. After continuing to be distracted by the headwinds, I found myself discouraged. I was looking forward to a positive run that day and now I was captivated by discouragement. It hit me that I could either give in to my discouragement or I could be determined to get my focus back on my run and my distance goal. That's what I did. I made a decision and I conquered discouragement with a renewed focus and determination on my goal! This became a positive and powerful Life Coaching tip that will stay with me for a very long time.

There will be chapters, seasons and situations in your life that will be challenging. With those challenges, there will be great temptation to get distracted. Distractions, if not dealt with, often lead to discouragement. When distraction and discouragement come knocking at your door, simply reply "You are not welcome here!". Fight hard to not allow life's "headwinds" to become a distraction and get you discouraged. Individuals who stay determined and press on are those who **<u>Live Above Average</u>**!

Coaching Tip 49

Spread Encouragement

Words have the power to influence, either for the positive or for the negative. There will be times in your life when you or others may wonder if you can accomplish a task that may seem unachievable. At that moment, words of encouragement are needed. Some of the most powerful words that others can say to you or you can say to yourself are "You Can Do It"! It's amazing how powerful these words can be to encourage, inspire and motivate. Great things can happen when you hear and believe "You Can Do It"!

One of the problems in all of this is that there can be other voices, even your own, that says "You Can't Do It!" It's amazing how destructive and discouraging these words can be. They can "take the wind out of your sails". Often when facing challenges that seem huge or overwhelming, words of doubt and disbelief enter. Don't allow "You Can't Do It" to negatively influence you.

There are three very important perspectives here that must be considered. First, seek out and surround yourself with people who are positive and will encourage you consistently with the words "You Can Do It"! Without this supportive group, it is highly unlikely you can do it on your own. You need people who believe in you and will consistently give you the positive affirmation you need to accomplish great things. Second, be very aware and very careful that you do not fall trap to the thoughts or words "You Can't Do It". These thoughts and words can creep in and negatively influence you.

Third, become a source of encouragement to others by consistently saying to them, "You Can Do It". The principle is true, give and it shall be given to you. If you need and expect others to encourage you, you need to be willing and available to encourage them as well. When you live in a world of encouragement, it is amazing how many great and remarkable things you can accomplish. Individuals who spread encouragement are those who who **Live Above Average!**

Coaching Tip 50

Finish Well

Every journey starts with a first step! It is important for any goal, project or agenda to get a good start. If you start off poorly, negatively or insufficiently, you often have to play the catch-up game. An even more important reality is how you finish. How you finish is more important than how you start. Have you ever watched a sporting event where an individual or team fell far behind in the beginning only to end up winning in the end? It was not how the event started, but how it ended that made the difference.

When you review your past, how well did you finish certain projects, opportunities, endeavors or events? You will probably be able to see how you finished some well and others not so well. Celebrate that you finished some well and don't be too hard on yourself for those that you didn't finish well. You can't change the past, but you can improve in the future.

Here are a few keys to finishing well. First, finishing well requires that you are extremely clear on what the goal or the desired end result will be. People don't finish well because they are not clear on these. Think about some of your key goals or projects and make sure that you are extremely clear on what it is you are trying to achieve, obtain and accomplish. Second, accept that challenges, detours, and roadblocks are often a part of the journey. Anticipate them. It would be foolish and naive to think the journey to your goals or the desired end result will be easy or without these. When they come, don't let them surprise or unsettle you.

Managing your expectations in this regard is very important in finishing well.

Finally, never give up on your dreams! Dedicate yourself to a no give-up, no give-in mentality. When you feel discouraged, dedicate yourself to continue to not give up or give in. When you feel like throwing in the towel, continue to push through. When you feel like it's just not worth it anymore, persevere. Remember, how you finish is often more important than how you start. Individuals who finish well are those who **Live Above Average!**

Thank You's

I am a very fortunate and blessed man to have so many family and friends who have helped me on my life's journey. I sincerely want to thank each and every individual that I have had the privilege to meet and know over the years.

Let me begin with a special "Thank You" to my parents, Bob Crabtree and Jean Frederick. I love you both and thank you for all the love, encouragement and support you have provided me over the years! To my deceased step-father Larry Frederick, who was a successful business leader and taught me so much about leadership.

To the Churches and Ministries that I have had the privilege to serve over the past 40 years – First Christian Church of Fort Collins, CO; Victory Fellowship Church of Midwest City, OK; Christ Church Fellowship of Cincinnati, OH; Iasis Christ Fellowship of Fort Collins, CO; Life Church of Fort Collins, CO and Connections Church of Fort Collins, CO, the congregation that I currently serve.

Thank you to my special friend H.B. London, who has been a mentor and friend for many years. To the guys that I have looked up to as great spiritual friends and leaders – Blake, Bob, Charlie, Chuck, Daryl, David, Doug, Drew, Gary, Grant, Greg, Kevin, Johnny, Randy, Rick, Rod, and Scott. To all those who wrote Endorsements for the book, you guys are awesome! To my dear and long-term friends John and Laurie Schmidt and Roger and Susie Sample. You guys have been a true support and inspiration to me over many years. To special friends Greg and Ellen Yancey who allowed me to get away to their lovely home in the Colorado Mountains to work on and finish up my writing.

To my awesome and incredible children who have been the joy and delight of my heart – Kyle Crabtree of Dallas, TX; Kristin Crabtree of Dallas, TX; Nathanael Crabtree of Fort Collins, CO. I am confident that all three of you are and will continue to be world changers and **Live Above Average.**

To my beloved wife of 35 years - Kathy Crabtree. Without your constant love, support, encouragement, partnership and prayers, none of this would have been possible. Thanks for being my closest friend and life partner!

Finally, to Almighty God and His Son Jesus Christ who have given me a hope, reason, and ability to **Live Above Average**!

Jeff Crabtree

Acknowledgments

First, a very special "Thank You" to my Co-Editor **Sarah Brase.** It was such an incredible pleasure to work with you on this project. Your sweet spirit, thoughtfulness, diligence, professionalism, communication skills and editing skills were exceptional. I could have never done it without you. You have a super future in front of you and it will be exciting to see all that is in store for you!

Second, a special "Thank You" to my awesome wife **Kathy,** who was also a Co-Editor. Your skill, patience, and assistance helped such a great deal. I so appreciate your wisdom and support throughout this process. I could have never gotten this far without your special partnership!

Finally, a very special "Thank You" to my graphic artist **Jim Hale.** Your professionalism in all that you do is impeccable. You have worked me on so many projects over the years and now your work on the book has helped a great deal. I'm thankful for your long-term friendship, as well as all the ways your artistic talents have assisted me with this book. I love your creativity!

About the Author
Jeff Crabtree

For the past 40 years, Jeff has devoted himself to helping people in regards to "<u>**Living Above Average**</u>" as a Senior Pastor, Church Planter, Denominational Executive and Personal Life Coach. Jeff's passion for Life Coaching began in 2005 when we founded Next Level Life Coaching in Fort Collins, Colorado. Jeff has counseled, encouraged and coached numerous people, helping them to clearly identify their goals and pathways for success. In this process, he has assited individuals and couples in learning and applying certain **Life Coaching Tips** that have catapulted many of them to live lives they never dreamed possible!

Jeff's passion is to help people understand the pathway and process to true success via the **Life Coaching Tips** he has developed. He strongly believes a person's full potential must be discovered and then developed. Jeff is married to his wife of 35 years, Kathy, and they have three adult children.

Please feel free to email Jeff with questions or to request volume quantities of this book at
<u>livingaboveaverage@yahoo.com</u>

96614235R00071

Made in the USA
Lexington, KY
22 August 2018